Perspectives
Children and Work
What Are the Issues?

Series Consultant: Linda Hoyt

Flying Start
to Literacy®

Contents

Children and work: is there a simple answer?

Children in Australia and New Zealand and many other countries benefit from laws that limit the number of hours a child may work.

But Save the Children – an international group that works with the United Nations – estimates that there are more than 115 million girls and boys in the world today who are engaged in work that is likely to be dangerous to their physical or mental health, or to interfere with their education.

Not all work is harmful. Many children and young people receive benefits from being economically active.

Is there a simple answer to the issue of children and work? Is it just a question of balance?

Childhood lost

Throughout history, most countries have allowed and even encouraged children to work. Author Mary-Anne Creasy explains how the way in which children worked has changed over time and the movements that campaigned to protect children from being exploited in factories and coal mines.

Why did some people try to make laws to protect children?

Farmers and their families in the fields at harvest time, 1869.

Up until the year 1750, most families in England lived and worked on farms. Their children also worked on these farms. If poor families lived in cities, many boys worked as chimney sweeps, or as messengers, or were sent away from home to learn a trade. Many girls left home at age 12 to work as servants or learn dressmaking.

From the late 1750s, power-driven machines replaced people on farms, and families were forced to move to cities to find work. Factories were built everywhere, first in England and then in the United States, and many children were sent by their parents to work in them. Factories needed coal to power the machines, so coal mines also employed children to haul heavy loads up narrow tunnels for 12 hours a day.

Farming families work on a farm in Colorado, USA, in 1915. Many of the workers were children under 14 years of age.

Wherever children were employed, their working conditions were dangerous. They worked in dark, dirty places, with no rest, for as many as 16 hours a day. In factories the machines had no safety guards, so injuries were a constant threat. In coal mines children became injured from carrying heavy loads long distances, and sick from breathing in the coal dust.

A group of child workers at a cotton weaving factory in Lancashire, England, 1910

Children worked for very low wages. They were nearly five times cheaper to employ than adults. They were also obedient and unlikely to protest about their poor conditions and low pay.

As the number of children working in factories and mines in England increased, some politicians and famous writers brought attention to the shameful conditions children were working in. Charles Dickens wrote *David Copperfield*; Lord Shaftesbury was responsible for the passing of the *Mines Act of 1842* that restricted the employment of children in mines. These people campaigned for the government to protect working children.

After many investigations and evidence provided by children, a series of laws were passed during the 1800s, first in the United Kingdom, then in Europe. These laws shortened the working hours for children and set out minimum ages that children could work. The United States took longer to pass laws to protect children; it was not until the 1930s that labour was regulated for children under 16.

Unlike Europe and the United States, in Australia and New Zealand not many children were employed. This was because there were not as many factories or the work available was not suited for children. Strong, skilled workers, such as brickmakers, boiler-makers or engineers were needed.

Both Australia and New Zealand depended on cattle for food, sheep for exporting wool, or mining in remote regions. The cattle and sheep farms and stations and the coal mines were a long way from any towns, where families with children lived. Children just could not perform these jobs.

Kids fight back

In this article, Jill Silos-Rooney tells us about brave children who took a stand to stop not only themselves from being exploited, but others as well.

What would you have done?

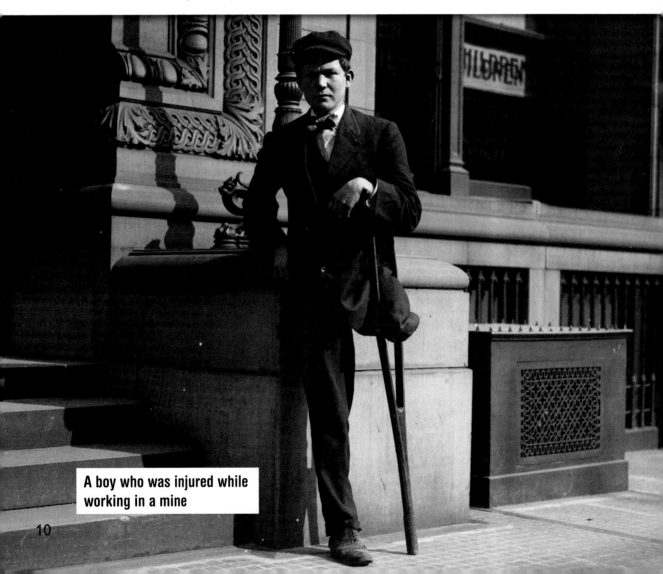

A boy who was injured while working in a mine

Most people don't think much about the roles that children have played in history. By 1900, over two million children under the age of 16 in the United States had spent part of their childhood working in terrible conditions. In the beginning, there were no laws or regulations to protect children who worked in these places. Employers could also get away with paying children much less than adult workers.

Workplaces could be dangerous. The hours were long. Children worked with huge, heavy machines. They sometimes suffered severe injuries. Children usually had to stop going to school – it was the only way to keep their jobs.

For all these reasons, many children actively protested. They fought for better working conditions, higher pay and fewer hours.

Young female mill workers in Lowell, Massachusetts in the United States, went on strike in 1836. When the mill owners reduced the workers' wages, the workers protested. Eventually the workers asked people to sign petitions to support their cause. They also created the Lowell Female Labor Reform Association. It was the first women's labour union in the United States.

Children also fought against unfair work conditions in New York City. Newspaper boys went on strike there in 1899. These "newsies" fought back when newspaper owners Joseph Pulitzer and William Randolph Hearst raised the price of papers. Newsies had to buy the papers that they sold to the public. Higher newspaper prices made it harder for newsies to make money. The owners also refused to buy back any unsold papers.

Louis Ballat was a 14-year-old newsie. He was known as "Kid Blink" because he was blind in one eye. He rallied the other newsboys and they went on strike. The owners were angry, but the newsboys did get the owners to buy back any unsold papers. This way the newsies didn't lose money.

Children who worked in factories refused to accept poor conditions. They fought the business owners. They helped win more workers' rights, better pay and better work conditions.

Young "newsies"

Two young girls protesting child labourers

Rights of the child

In 1989, the General Assembly of the United Nations adopted the Convention on the Rights of the Child (CRC). The Convention outlines the rights all children should have – at home, at school and in the community. The countries that signed the Convention, which include Australia and New Zealand, have a duty to ensure that children's rights are protected through regulation and laws.

Article 32 of the Convention focuses on work and the rights of the child. Why does the CRC think children need to be protected?

ARTICLE 32

1. States Parties recognise the right of the child to be protected from economic exploitation and from performing any work that is likely to be hazardous or to interfere with the child's education, or to be harmful to the child's health or physical, mental, spiritual, moral or social development.

2. States Parties shall take legislative, administrative, social and educational measures to ensure the implementation of the present article. To this end, and having regard to the relevant provisions of other international instruments, States Parties shall in particular:

(a) Provide for a minimum age or minimum ages for admission to employment;

(b) Provide for appropriate regulation of the hours and conditions of employment;

(c) Provide for appropriate penalties or other sanctions to ensure the effective enforcement of the present article.

Chocolate from children

Chocolate is a popular snack food in many countries around the world. But, as Deb Dun explains, many people don't know that children in West Africa pick most of the world's cocoa beans. Cocoa is the main ingredient in chocolate.

Why do children have to work on cocoa farms?
Can we do anything to help them?

Imagine this. Ten-year-old Sametta lives in Cote d'Ivoire (or Ivory Coast), a country in West Africa. She wakes up at 4 a.m., eats millet porridge and then walks three kilometres to her family's cocoa bean field. For the next 12 hours, she picks cocoa pods and then breaks them open. She scoops out the 30 to 50 seeds, or "beans", that are inside the pods. (About 800 beans are needed to make one kilogram of chocolate.)

Sametta does not have time to go to school. Her family needs her to work in order for them to survive. Her health is also at risk because the cocoa pods are sprayed with poisonous pesticides.

This is not a story from long ago. This is happening right now. Every day in Ivory Coast, Ghana, Nigeria and Cameroon, about 300,000 children pick cocoa beans that will be sold to big chocolate companies.

Most of the children work on their families' farms. They need to sell every bean to make money for their families to survive. School is out of the question.

Why is this happening? The reason is money. Families who own the cocoa bean farms are very poor. They depend on growing and selling cocoa beans to survive. Without help from their children, the farmers would not be able to buy food. Big chocolate companies pay farmers a very low price for their cocoa beans. Most farmers earn only between $30 and $100 a year.

For some children, the situation is even worse. Children from some extremely poor countries in Africa are sent to work in other countries where cocoa beans grow. In exchange, their government is paid. About 6000 of these children are slaves. They sleep in dirty rooms, work 12-hour days without pay, are fed very little and are sometimes whipped.

A 13-year-old boy in West Africa spreads out cocoa beans to dry.

Cocoa farmers open up cocoa pods to extract the cocoa.
Farmers help each other with their harvests.

Still, there is some hope. There are organisations around
the world that work to eliminate child labour. For example,
a group of farmers in Africa and South America are called
Fairtrade Certified. Companies that buy cocoa beans from
these farmers sign an agreement. They promise to pay the
farmers a Fairtrade price. This is enough for them to buy
food and clothing for their families and send their children
to school. There are about 45,000 farmers in this program.
Any chocolate made from these farmers' beans is labelled
Fairtrade.

You can help eliminate child labour too, by looking for the
Fairtrade trust mark when you shop for chocolate.

Family helpers or child farmers?

In this article, Claire Halliday explains that for many children growing up on rural farms today, doing hard, physical work to help their parents is still a normal part of childhood.

What do you think is the right balance?
How much work is too much?

Many hands to help

For children growing up on farms, helping their mothers and fathers with the chores before and after school is part of their daily lives. The chores often include milking cows, harvesting crops and doing the hard work needed to keep the animals fed and the farmland healthy and productive.

Child labour laws

There is a difference between children who work on family farms to lend a hand, and children who are forced to work on farms in order to survive. In Australia and New Zealand, there are laws that regulate the age and number of hours that children can work. Children under the age of 12 can work on their families' farms or in family businesses if they have their parents' permission. The only exception is that they can't work during school hours.

The balance between work and fun

While it is clear that very young children should not be doing work that puts them in direct danger, their help on family farms can make a huge difference to a family's income.

By feeding animals, looking after fields or even fixing fences, children who work on the farm can help their parents save money.

Fair work

Hopefully, you help your family around the house – making your bed, looking after your pets or putting the rubbish out.

Imagine the chores you might be expected to do if you lived on a farm. What work would you be happy to do to help your family grow food for other people to buy and enjoy? It's something to think about next time you eat your favourite food and imagine how it made its way to your table.

What is your opinion?: How to write a persuasive argument

1. State your opinion

Think about the issues related to your topic. What is your opinion?

2. Research

Research the information you need to support your opinion.

Related PERSPECTIVES book   Internet   Other sources

3. Make a plan

Introduction

How will you "hook" the reader?

State your opinion.

List reasons to support your opinion.

What persuasive devices will you use?

Reason 1	**Reason 2**	**Reason 3**
Support your reason with evidence and details.	Support your reason with evidence and details.	Support your reason with evidence and details.

Conclusion

Restate your opinion. Leave your reader with a strong message.

4. Publish

Publish your persuasive argument.

Use visuals to reinforce your opinion.